The Witchid Good Energy of

Hickory

"to release that which no longer serves and reshape anew"

Myth Magik
~Carya~

She who became the aspect of STRENGTH in the Goddess, ARTEMIS

By T.L. Woodliff

Crystal Heart Imprints

FROM THE
RECLAIMING TRADITION

Fire becomes the potential for harvest—to bring forth that which has been planted and nurtured within.

—Ruth Souther *The Elemental Priestess*

Sacred fire that shapes this land,
Summer teacher, winter friend,
Protect us as we learn anew
To work, to heal, to live with you.
Green, green crown
Roots underground.
Kissed by fire,
Still growing higher.

—Starhawk *The Earth Path*

How To Use This Book

With each exercise, you are encouraged to look at your issue from a new perspective using the guidance of the sacred energy of the *Hickory* or the path of *Carya*: Earth energy and mythical guidance working together to establish the transforming power of Fire.

Traditional psychological and witchid explorations in writing, visualization, chanting and working with the Sacred Elements is complimented with modern tools available to most.

Use these as a year-and-a-day practice, a lunar cycle of awareness, or as needed; move through these at your own pace. I encourage you not to rush through these as something to complete but to look at each as something to explore.

At the end, you will burn or bury the pen and the book. It is a release of stored energy. In doing so, you follow the guidance of the Hickory in shedding its leaves and nuts to make space and energy, to rest, and then to grow in new ways once the spring calls.

When you bury these items, you bury all judgments against YOU and others, shedding once and for all what needs to fall to the Earth to be reshaped into something new.

POWER OF THE GREEN WORLD
Sacred Hickory

Blessings of Artemis,
who saw a savage strength in Carya and
claimed her as an aspect of the divine feminine.

I, Hickory, Carya incarnate, savior
of nations, bid you now to release
that which no longer serves:
- *YOUR HEART*
- *YOUR STRENGTH*
- *YOUR DESIRES*
- *YOUR WORLD VIEW*
- *YOUR CREATIVE SOUL*

Leave all to me! Give this energy back to the Mother of us all.

Allow her to consume and RESHAPE it. Walk with me this day and longer. Walk in the Green World. Walk with the forests of the Earth and rejoice in the magik of Life.

Become the HedgeWitch, the Healer, Wise Woman & Male Mystic combined; all aspects of the divine. Seek the Wisdom of the Green World.

Plant your feet in both realms.

id

/id/

noun

PSYCHOANALYSIS

    1. the personality component made up of unconscious psychic energy to satisfy
       basic desires using the pleasure principle.

"the conflict between the drives of the id and the demands of the cultural superego"

witch·id

/ wiCHid/

adjective

PSYCHIC-AWARENESS

    1. psychical awareness and ability to use baddassery when required.

"She showed witchid good sense"

    2. one who walks in harmony with the Earth
       Similar: excellent" superb"first-rate"first-class"superior

To Artemis, to Earth & Fire, and to Yourself
Set Your Intention:

INTRODUCTION

Before we even say hello, **GO BACK** to the previous page and write your goal in an *active* voice. Write it in the box. Take time to underline it, add stars, or go over it in bold strokes. Make it clear what you intend to do by adding your emotions.

*DESIRE TO CHANGE   *A NEED FOR HEALING

Whatever emotions have moved you to begin this work, even if it seems simple, such as curiosity, bring them in. Make them a part of the intentional statement.

And be specific. Make sure to word it in such a way that the action is about **you**, even if you were not responsible for bringing this issue into your life. *You can't magik someone else into clarity*. But you can choose to provide your Sacred Self with action in *everything* that affects you.

Examples:

"*I wish to understand my reactions*" is too vague.

"**I need to understand why I get so hurt when she doesn't listen to me**" is specific.

"*I will learn to release my anger*" is good, but…
"**I will release my anger at his lack of interest in my art**" is clearer.

"*I release anxiety*" is too general.
"**I will release expectations about my work peers and be at peace in my day-to-day workday**" shifts the focus off of others and onto what you can control.

Finally, if you are unclear about what to say, fill the edges in with images or words around your emotional reality. The work that follows helps to clarify the actual root of the issue. Don't be surprised if you need to change the wording more than one time. Scribble on it; make question marks and angry symbols; talk to it out loud; paint/color/spit on it. It's yours. That's the point of a burn book. When you don't know what to say, express in blobs of paint, tears, colors, or layers of things like paper, cloth or seeds from the soil.

And now, **Hello**! Thank you for being here. In each section, you'll be prompted to journal, act or in some way look at this issue anew as we follow the ancient story of Carya, a woman who, because of *her* choices in how she reacted to events out of her control, became the aspect of **strength** in the Goddess, Artemis.

Using the sacred energy of the Hickory tree —her tree—as our guide, we will seek out and EMBRACE that moment when you first respond with reluctance to sit with the topic. Why? Because **that's** the place where you'll work your magik, my friend.

Welcome to the Green World way of living, learning, growing and manifesting the changes you desire.

Magik: The ability to shape your consciousness at will.

MYTH & MAGIK

Myths are the lessons of morality, the passing on of knowledge, time used for community and personal growth in compassion and wisdom.

Take from the myth the understanding that human struggles connect us all. Stories told around a campfire in ancient Siberia _can be as relevant today_ as any book of new psychology **if** you take the effort to place yourself into the lesson being conveyed. At its root, magik is the effort to do the work of psychological change: build intuition through practice and trust; seek manifestations of desire through strength of will; to grow through the lessons that Nature provides and the sharing of them through myths.

Carya's Ancient Myth, Reclaimed

Carya was the daughter of a king in ancient Greece. Her family had the duty of hosting great *feasts to honor the gods—gods who attended personally. Apollo was given much reverence by her city, and he blessed her and her sisters because of it.*

Carya attended one feast that was held to honor Dionysus, the god of wine and merriment.

The story splits at this point, telling one thing in one place and time and another thing at another place and time. All are relevant. All had purpose for the listeners. The version that is relevant here is this one:

Carya's blessings and mannerisms attracted the god Dionysus, known for revelry and wine. She spurred his attentions and her sisters raced to her aid, seeking to keep her hidden from his divine sight. He turned them all into stone.

In her devastation, Carya still refused him and tried to end her life rather than submit. The god changed her into a nut tree, not allowing her to ever escape.

Apollo's twin sister, the goddess Artemis, saw. Though this was her brother's city, she was moved to visit the Lady of the Nut Tree and **claim** *what she observed as a savage, womanly* *strength, forever after to be an aspect of her divinity. Carya was immortalized and merged with the Goddess.*

A Caryatid Statue
The Lady of the Nut Tree
Many temples and buildings of
ancient Greece are supported
by the strength of Carya.

Carya's Priestesses

The Priestesses of Carya were called the *caryatidai*, and each year women performed a dance called the *caryatis* at a festival in honor of Artemis Carya.

She is still honored to this day! *Caryatids Ancient Greek Dance Company of Dora Stratou Theater* is named after her and performs their version of the caryatis.

Visit here to read an incredible accounting of how the Carya is alive today as women dance in her honor.

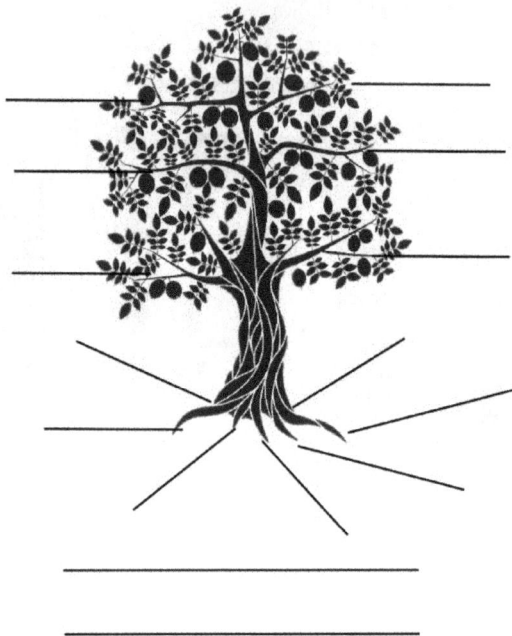

Hickory is the genus *Carya,* from the same family as walnuts. Pecans are a species of hickory, native to North America.

Wherever you live, the myth of Carya is accessible to you: Strength is found every time you see the sacred energy of the tree, create an offering to Artemis, or invoke and honor the memory of Carya. The next time you see a pecan tree... remember her and accept the strength she freely offers.

FIRST
QUESTIONS

SIT IN SILENCE AND INVITE CARYA'S
STRENGTH TO BE WITH YOU. BE
FIERCE IN YOUR QUEST FOR CHANGE &
UNDERSTANDING. HONESTY AND TIME
ARE REQUIRED TO MOVE YOU FORWARD.

Remember- this book is to be either buried or
burned at the end, leaving nothing for others
to find or your future self to feel guilty about.
This is the beginning of releasing that which
binds you.

1) HOW LONG HAS THIS ISSUE
WEIGHED ON YOUR MIND?

2)   HOW HAS IT AFFECTED YOUR LIFE? YOUR GOALS?

*

*

*

*

*

*

*

*

*

*

*

*

*

3) DO YOU HAVE SUPPORT IN YOUR LIFE AS YOU WORK TO CLAIM THIS CHANGE?

BE DETAILED HERE. LIST OUT EVERYTHING THAT SUPPORTS YOU, AND _EVERYTHING_ THAT TAKES YOUR TIME AND ENERGY BUT DOES NOT PROVIDE YOU WITH AN EQUAL AMOUNT OF SUPPORT.

*

*

*

*

*

*

*

*

*

*

*

*

*

*

*

*

*

*

*

*

*

4)BY STARTING, YOU *HAVE* ALREADY
CHANGED. WHAT BROUGHT THIS

ABOUT? WHY NOW?

Deeper Clarity

TRUE UNDERSTANDING TAKES TIME

In the myth of Carya, she begins with the simple act of attending a feast. In doing this, she honored the traditions of her ancestors. She could neither undo this step nor foresee the results of her actions. It is the truth in every decision we make each day.

Go to page ten and look at the Hickory tree. Think of it as your source of strength: it connects you with the aspect of Carya that Artemis made divine.

Thinking of your issue, what were the roots that brought it into creation? Use "I admit" phrases as often as possible. Yes, it is true that things happen that are completely out of our control, just like the god of revelry's relentless pursuit of Carya, but the lesson is in how Carya responded to the realities she faced. "I admit" can be an extremely powerful tool toward release if you're willing to focus on only what you have power over, and analyzing your role in them.

I admit, this exists in my life because:

_____

_____

_____

_____

_____

_____

_____

_____.

And that is because:

_____

_____

_____

_____

_____

_____

_____

_____

_____.

I admit:

_____

_____

_____

_____

_____

_____

_____

_____

_____

_____.

Do your best to go at least *seven layers* into this.

STEP ONE: Write words along those roots of the tree on page ten—create seven spaces on the roots.

I admit:

_____

_____

_____

_____

_____

_____

_____

_____

———————————————————————————

————————————————————————.

I admit:

———————————————————————————

———————————————————————————

———————————————————————————

———————————————————————————

———————————————————————————

———————————————————————————

———————————————————————————

————————————————————————.

I admit:

———————————————————————————

_____

_____

_____

_____

_____

_____

_____

_____.

I admit:

_____

_____

_____

_____

_____

—————————————————————

—————————————————————

—————————————————————

—————————————————————

———————————————————·

STEP TWO: **Now look to the branches. What has it caused in your life, and also in the world?** List six results of this issue being a part of your life and those you care about.

STEP THREE: **On the two lines under the tree,** write one sentence to summarize the roots of the issues, and one sentence to summarize the results. Think of these roots and results as coming from only your perspective. As had been said, you can't magik others into clarity. But you can look at how you've fueled or ignored a situation too long, or have simply been too afraid to change.

7+6+2=15=1+5=6   Six is the energetic

number of divine messages. Receive them to bring balance toward living a desired life, both physically and emotionally: the higher self and conscious self in harmony.

My own journey with the sacred aspects of the Hickory tree concerned self-judgements. I had a dance studio I closed to focus on my other work. Was it ever a success? The roots were certainly planted in the goal of financial success, in part. But I realized I never fed those roots as much as the others. I worked harder on 'community' and thus, they led to strong branches. My students now teach. Classes that began there continue and have created their own trees. A forest of community was created, yet I judged myself harshly for not feeding that 'other' root more.

STEP FOUR: Look at your own root and branch relationships again. Go back to the image of the tree with your words written there, or take these thoughts out into nature and look at a towering tree. Can you see what roots you nourished to grow certain branches? Can you celebrate the ones you didn't even realize supported others? Release your judgment, and focus now on the emotion of longing.

DESIGN YOUR LONGING FOR CHANGE WITH SIGIL MAGIK

Sigils are lines and curves. That's it. UNLESS YOU GIVE THEM MEANING, they are no different than a day spent doodling in the margins of the paper instead of taking notes. It is *a seal* on your intent.

Intention becomes key. A chevron means to *change directions* because you give it that *focused* intention. The art of Witchcraft has always included the practice of the eyes and hands providing physical, Earth realities to the nonphysical aspects of the mind, the spirit and the endless unknown.

To create sigils, you can follow patterns

that others have made before you; some of them quite ancient. There are many books available if you wish to use such symbols. You can create your own pattern, where each swirl or line has a definite meaning, one that you chant into creation, channel with meditation or drum into life. Or, you can use the moon's phases to 'charge' and support your work.

On the next page, you'll see some of my sigils. For some, I doodled. Others, I took images and cut segments out, adding lines and dots and swirls where I wanted them. One of them was purchased from another witch, the symbol infused with the intention they set. I added the element of music to help me concentrate—frame drums playing a steady heartbeat.

When I was traveling on the East Coast for a few months on a book tour, I created a sigil—prosperity and protection. The week I returned home, the sigil fell from the necklace that I had worn every day of that journey. Its work was done.

There's a wonderful, FREE tutorial on YouTube if you wish to follow a more formulated style. (I like this one because it's rooted in psychology and similar to my own practice, but I do lines to represent syllables as opposed to using the letters.)

Here are examples of how they can look. What's fascinating is that the intention you start with may reshape itself somewhat. After you've worked through several sections, go back and see if it needs to change as you have changed.

Another way to think of this work is that you in your conscious state are leaving breadcrumbs for your unconscious state to follow. The two parts rarely converse easily. Symbols help to bridge the gap.

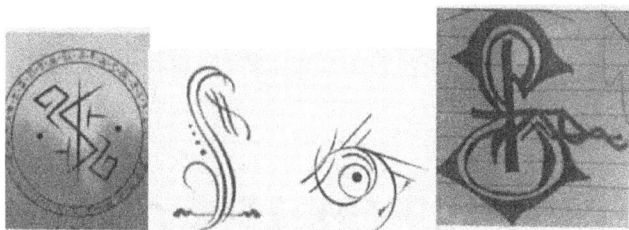

At the beginning of your work with this burn book, a sigil becomes the visual representation of what may or may not have words yet. Focus on your *longing* for change. Design something that you want to step into and bask in a glorious feeling of ease. If you can't think of how to start, use Carya's tree as your foundation. Mark your intention into this book by placing it **here:**

THE STORIES OF WITCHES

Root the issue in the ground, and also bind your story to the Winds of the Earth to capture and store for all the ages, adding to our collective wisdom.

Oral stories are in our DNA. Our ancestors used them to teach, to warn and to inspire.

Write **your** story about this issue *as a folktale* with a beginning, middle and, possibly, the end. If it's not time to write the end, come back to it. You are free to make is as simple as you like, or to create great characters or scenes based only in your imagination.

DON'T BE FOOLED—this may sound simple, but rewriting an ending is a powerful psychological tool of dealing with grief. And writing the story as a fable provides distance and a new perspective. There is power in creating your own, mythic story. In the story of Carya, I shared the gods' interests and power, Carya's family, her traditions ... All in just a few lines. How does your story play out in the greater scheme of myth and magik?

ONCE UPON A TIME:

_____

_____

_____

_____

_____

_____

_____

_____

_____

_____

_____

_____

_____

_____

_____

_____

_____

_____

_____

THE MIDDLE:

_____

_____

_____

_____

_____

_____

_____

_____

_____

_____

_____

_____

_____

_____

_____

_____

_____

_____

_____

THE END:

_____

_____

_____

_____

_____

_____

_____

_____.

ROWAN MOON 10-DAY PRACTICE

While the Rowan moon is the full moon found in February, this is a practice that can be done at any time.

The Rowan moon is the symbol of *initiation.* And it is also the reminder to practice the art of *Astral Projection.*

You'll practice something daily to create a <u>ritual for self-initiation</u>. Self-initiation is a practice of the Reclaiming Tradition. We do not follow hierarchical tiers like some traditions, but instead gauge our own growth or needs by self-reflection and a deeper connection with the Wild.

There are several reasons I chose a self-initiation practice for this burn book:

1- You are reshaping your life through intention and will. That deserves a moment of respect.

2- Carya was denied this option. We honor her by bringing her into this practice with us, allowing her energies to bask in the freedom she was denied.

The key for this practice is that **the very first time** you feel the urge to *not* do it, or to put it off for later, **stop**. *Write* instead. Ask yourself why? You are in the moment and no reason is too small. List everything that blocked you from *being excited* to practice and strengthen a habit to develop this magical skill.

The bow of Artemis is lovingly polished.
This is a skill in which she rejoices!

One week, tens days, or a lunar month of daily practice in this art, **or another that calls to you,** is an excellent way to acknowledge self-initiation. We are using ten days because it represents freshness and new beginnings.

ROWAN MOON INITIATION PRACTICE

HOW: Choose a time of day to consistently practice. Set the timer each day for ten minutes. Close your eyes, follow your breath. With each inhale, visualize your consciousness rising above your physical form, going higher each time.

Seek the energy in a cord of light that keep you connected to your body. Don't stress about finding it. Instead, be open to discovery while you keep following the breath and continue to visualize yourself rising.

When the timer rings, it's time to follow the cord home.

Did you at any time in this ten-day challenge stall or put it off for later? **Y   N**

I Paused Because:

10-Day Ten-Minute Practice Observations:

FAMILIARS

Artemis raced through the woods with her pack of seven hounds guiding her. Pallas Athena's Owl is said to have rested on the shoulder of her blind side and enabled her to see the whole truth.

The human connection with animals is a powerful bond.

Now think of the owl, perched and watching the world below. She is not caught up in the emotions of those she observes. She can see from a different perspective.

It is time for you to do the same.

1. Write about your issue as if a traveling wise woman observed you, an ancient philosopher... What would she describe from her view on the road?
2. Invite her in for coffee. Would her view of the situation change? Do you think she would offer any advice?
3. Allow yourself to look at the animals in

your life with new eyes. Look at yourself through theirs. Look at the world around you. Open yourself to viewing the world through the eyes of every creature you meet.

We humans often forget that we are not alone on this planet. Taking the time to look at yourself through the eyes of your pets, the birds who visit your home, the animal kingdom around you is to grow in your own magik.

WHAT WOULD A PASSING WISE WOMAN SAY ABOUT THE SITUATION AT FIRST GLANCE?

WHAT WOULD SHE SAY AFTER GETTING TO KNOW YOU AND HEARING YOUR THOUGHTS?

OBSERVE YOURSELF THROUGH THE EYES OF NATURE AND THE ANIMAL WORLD:

JOURNEY WITH CARYA

It's time to honor the transformation of Carya with one of your own. This intensifies your commitment to change and creates an energy bond between the two of you.

After following the first three steps below, go back to the short line under each of the three lines and write "change me" to deepen your connection with your words.

> 1. Draw your sigil and allow for any changes it wants. Look at your image for a few moments with deep breaths.
> 2. Add the Sacred Element of Water— your pure emotional response to this issue. Wrap your sigil in those feelings.

3. Write a three-line poem, prayer, spell or gratitude that deals with your issues.

_____

_____

_____

_____

_____

_____

4. Chant the three lines as you stare into the ball, **supported** by your sigil.

5. Write the words on a piece of paper and wrap it around a glass.

6. Visualize the Sacred Water you called now in the glass and pulling in the vibrations of your words. Pour physical water into the glass. Place it in the fridge.

7. Drink the next day. With each swallow, visualize both waters permeating every cell in your body. Accept the transformation.

**REMAKE YOUR SIGIL NEXT TO THE
SPIRAL AND SOFTEN YOUR EYES AS YOU
CHANT THE WORDS YOU CRAFTED.**

CHANGE YOUR POV

Active Visualizations

Think about Carya's point of view (POV) at three distinct, single moments:

1) When she heads to the feast, filled with excitement.

2) When she makes a choice to tell the god NO.

3) As the Hickory tree, providing life-giving nuts to her community. Pause here, close your eyes and *see* her.

Visualize your issue at three points. Choose them.

1)

2)

3)

Now, observe these **three points from the perspective of three people you value**, *even if you don't know them.*

Visualize an actual conversation with each, on each of the chosen points. You may write insights down as you wish, *but this is a visualization practice.* You may choose to write symbols instead of words, or images instead of feelings.

OBSERVATIONS- Allow yourself to be harsh, ugly and raw in this segment. Even if you know something isn't real, sometimes writing out our nagging thoughts will help you to *know* they are not real.

Identify them so they no longer have any part of your future.

THE FIRST POINT IN YOUR STORY & WHY IT FEELS SIGNIFICANT:

THE SECOND POINT YOU CHOSE & WHY:

THE THIRD POINT:

SHIFT YOUR VIBRATION

Artist, author and Metaphysician, Teri Freesmeyer, is a well-known healer and member of many metaphysical, Earth-based and energy-focused events as a power-filled facilitator. Her Earthy blending of humor and truth led her to create an entire series of personal work with the topic, *Be Your Own Vibrator.*

Vibration is one of the cornerstones of all energy work. Everything in the universe has a vibration. Everything.
NOTE: If you ever have a chance to take a workshop with a true Yogi on the creation of "OHM," take it! It can be life changing.

Give and Receive a New Rhythm
Create a chant. Sing from the solar plexus. Find what notes FEEL good in you. **This is an**

offering.

- Step one: Pick a topic, such as *Growth, Insight, Creativity, Increased Intuition.*
- Step two: If this is your first time working on a chant, keep it simple. Write a two-line poem.
- Step three: Drum a rhythm. Give yourself time to relax into the sound. It doesn't matter what you drum with—your fingers on a tabletop are excellent tools.
- Step four: Make sounds and find notes that capture your feeling on this topic. Try chanting your words without notes at first, if that feels better. You don't have to sing to chant.

Example using a chant of mine:

> The Green Man of the Woods Came to Me.
> As I was walking beneath budding leaves,
> The Green Man of the Woods Came to Me.
> And this . . . is what . . . he said. (Ah, but that's a tale for another time!)

Now it's time to receive a new vibration. Sit, as Carya, in her transformed existence as the Hickory tree.

People would come and sing to her, giving praise for all that she brought to the world.

You, too, are worthy of receiving. You are here, on this planet. Practice accepting what is freely offered.

Choose a specific number of days. I'll leave it to you this time. You may wish to choose a number that has significant meaning to you, or you may wish to research numerology before choosing. BE INTENTIONAL WITH THIS CHOICE. Make sure it has some meaning to you.

It's a simple process, so no fears about biting off more than you can chew: Watch a chant on YouTube (or your other sources) and then *immediately go outside*, <u>eyes going to a distant item to focus upon (such as high leaves of a tree)</u> and **sit with the chant for five minutes**, in silence as it sings in your mind. Absorb the offering in silence as it echoes through your soul.

Power-filled Chants you might choose to use from YouTube:

*THE NEW CHEROKEE MORNING SONG WITH TRANSLATION posted by Seirios15

*ANILAH- MEDICINE CHANT; posted in 2014

*HYMN TO THE MUSE- Layne Redmond
(This is an **actual song used in ancient times.** It's worth the time to read Layne's writings.)

LAKOTA LULLABY Lakota Song Cover by Alexia Evellyn

HUMMING by Enya

I personally use the Hymn to the Muse often. The drums and spiraling voices echo in my heart for hours after each listen. Knowing this was an actual song used in the temples of old takes me to a different place and allows me to see my situation from a different perspective. Using the space below, write after each time you go outside. Remember, listen first and then go outside without the recording.

_____

_____

_____

_____

_____

_____

_____

_____

_____

_____

_____

_____

_____

_____

_____

_____

_____

_____

_____

_____

_____

_____

_____

_____

_____

_____.

LOOK FORWARD

It is **time to look beyond** this difficult time. I suggest taking a lunar month to work with the moon as you practice. Embrace and/or expand upon your talents in divination.

This shadows the work of Carya, the Lady of the Nut Tree, who knew what was needed of her in the coming year to be of service to her people in her tree form.

*Talk to the Higher Self
*Listen **and practice** the art of expanding intuition
*See the clues in everyday aspects of life where **your Green World Self is trying to communicate with you.**

These suggested methods of practice are just that—suggestions. If you desire to work on a particular skill, then do so and come back to these suggestions another time. The point is to make time to grow your intuition. A stronger connection to your intuition and your Higher Self will allow you to see the warnings ahead of things that may cause you harm: harm to self from others, harm to self from self, and harm to others, even if unintentional.

Allow it space in your life. I strongly suggest a timer.

SCRYING

Week One: Three times this week, gaze into a candle flame, each time lasting longer than the first. Ease into the practice. Only follow your breath that first day. This is to practice the art of RELEASE. No expectations.

Week Two: Make note of ALL coincidences you detect this week. Write them down, no matter how small: synchronicity is an unacknowledged part of our world! On the LAST day of the week, return to the candle. Release. We are honing intuition and the conscious mind must quiet. Expectations do not serve this process. Relax, let go.

Week Three: Continue marking the coincidences of life this week, but change that thinking into use of the word synchronicity and erase the word 'coincidence.' You do not need to write things this week, but pause and give them a true **mental** acknowledgment. (And a smile —they are a gift of your intuition.) *ADD A MIRROR* to your work with the candle magik. Play with the positioning of it. Continue the release of expectations.

Week Four: Place the mirror to the side of your space, and gaze into water. Use a very thin layer on a plate one day, a deep dark bowl on another. Again, change the lighting. Observe with focus and on this week, **change your mental shift to one of eager expectations**. Smile! Be excited.

The key in adding a good expectation, which creates the energy you want to draw, is to have zero judgment on what then happens. If something is seen, *wonderful.* If nothing came to you, then you spent time in sacred communion with elemental water. Still, *wonderful.*

SCRYING

COINCIDENCES

SYNCHRONICITY & CANDLE MAGIK

WATER WITH INTENTIONAL MENTAL SHIFT

THE ELEVENTH FIRE

In numerology, 11 is a Master number of higher intuition, stronger insights into the spiritual realm and a burst of energetic power.

In tarot, it is Justice: Truth, balance. **Fairness**.

It's time we honor the Sacred Element of Fire. Fire is our ability to transform. It is our passion to bring change. It is this element that gave Carya the ability to shift her entrapment by the petty god into a space where she provided nourishment to her people. Dionysus made her a tree. She created and provided the new food source, which we call the pecan.

This kind of energy is powerful. And it makes us sweat.

Sweat your prayers this week. Dance or drum yourself into **ecstasy**! Layne Redmond gifted us with Hymn to the Muse, an ancient song, refound and reaffirmed. When you dance without restriction, visualize the ancient priestesses and prophets dancing in sacred movement with you. Fuel each movement with the power of FIRE, setting your intention and then claiming it.

Dancing without direction and full freedom is a proven method to increase creativity. Let it also BURN away all doubts, and dance or drum from your place of power.

If you're not there already, tell yourself it is time, and go in with all guns blazing. YOU become the dance or the drum. YOU become the ability to transform your world. YOU become one with Fire. When you read the words, BODY*MIND*SPIRIT, this practice is the BODY. Now, YOU are the very fire of transformation!

Nothing calls in the Elemental Energy of Fire like full throttle, no holds barred dancing. Drums, bass, chanting—Whatever it is you do to find a rhythm, the transformational energy awaits one final explosion of your truest expression.

This is a thing near and dear to my heart. Trust me, you don't need to live in a large city where ecstatic dance events are held regularly. You just need some alone time, music that FEEDS your spirit and the desire to visualize the final outcome that you desire.

The Hickory drops its nuts and leaves to prepare for winter. To change. To be able to start anew in the spring. Fire calls to you to do the same. YOUR SWEAT becomes the leaves. Your chanting or hoots and shouts call to creation itself.

In one final blast of energetic release, you claim the ability to shed what held you back. You claim the ability to step onto your new path.

Ritualize this dance by giving shape to your shadow shelf. *See* the version of you that has lived only in your dreams. Dance beside this vision, with this vision, and then finally, merge and move together; one leading then the other, until you can no longer define a difference. Create sacred space with intention by adding candles, items from the natural world, pictures of ancestors and those you love and want to be strong for— everyone for whom you are doing this work.

It doesn't matter if you can't move your body. DANCE YOUR SPIRIT.

RITUAL BURNING OF RELEASE

Here is where you have brought yourself; this day belongs to you. As you answer these final questions, SEE the words joining together to form a cloak wrapped around your body.

1- TODAY, LOOK BACK AT THE FIRST PAGES. WHAT ARE YOUR FEELINGS ABOUT THIS ISSUE:

2-   WHAT   CHANGES   HAVE   YOU
MANIFESTED:

3- CAN YOU NOW BURY ANY LINGERING DOUBTS, JUDGEMENTS AND EMOTIONS THAT CONTROLLED YOU:

FINAL THOUGHTS THAT NEED TO GO:

_____

_____

_____

_____

_____

_____

_____

_____

.

RITUAL BURNING: STEPS

1) Bathe in water with Epsom salt or essential oils. Brush the water over every part of your body and say in command, I NOW RELEASE YOU. (May be

done without actual sound. Emotion and intent is key.)

2) Wear loose-fitting clothes to represent being fully seen under the night sky. (May be done skyclad.)

3) Dig a hole or set a fire as you chant the old words—The Earth, The Air, The Fire, The Water: Return, Return, Return, Return.

4) Peel the hickory wood from the book and say: I KEEP THIS TO REMEMBER. Place your book and pen onto the fire or into the hole and say: CARYA, SACRED ARTEMIS, MAY I STAND AS THE CARYATIDES OF OLD, HONORING YOU BOTH WITH MY RELEASE.

5) Watch the burn or fill the hole with dirt as you proclaim these words: I RELEASE ALL JUDGEMENTS OF MYSELF ON THIS ISSUE. WHAT IS DONE IS DONE. WHAT IS DECIDED IS DECIDED. AS I WILL, SO MOTE IT BE.

6) Place both hands on the top of the dirt or far above the flames and away from

any danger and VISUALIZE final strands of thought moving from your head and heart, through the center of your palms and into the flames and even the earth.

7)   Bury the ashes. Plant something as a symbol of regrowth over this when the season allows. Let the color, leaf or fragrance be something you find beautiful.

8)   IT IS DONE.